For Abe —

"It has
world, but time is all it
takes."

Seeing the Darkness

Naples, 1943-1945

All best, and thanks,

Bruce Cutler

3/23/98

Bruce Cutler

BkMk Press
THE UNIVERSITY OF MISSOURI–KANSAS CITY

Bruce Cutler

Afterlife (1997)

The Massacre at Sand Creek: Narrative Voices (1995)

Dark Fire (1985)

Nectar in a Sieve (1985)

The Maker's Name (1980)

The Doctrine of Selective Depravity (1980)

A Voyage to America (1967)

Sun City (1964)

A West Wind Rises (1962)

The Year of the Green Wave (1960)

Copyright © 1998 Bruce Cutler

No part of this book may be reproduced without written permission of the publisher. Please direct inquiries to:

BkMk Press of UMKC
University House
5100 Rockhill Road
Kansas City, MO 64110-2499

 Financial assistance for this book has been provided by the Missouri Arts Council, a state agency.

Cover art by Beth Thomas.

Cover design by Brad Kelley.
E-mail— coolgrafix@gvi.net
Internet— http://home.gvi.net/~coolgrafix/

Library of Congress Cataloging-in-Publication Data

Cutler, Bruce, 1930–
   Seeing the Darkness / Bruce Cutler.
      p.   cm.
   ISBN 1-886157-16-2 (acid-free paper)
   1. World War, 1939–1945--Italy--Naples--Poetry. I. Title.
PS3553.U8S44   1998
811'.54--dc21   97-44942
                                                                         CIP

This book was typeset in Times New Roman, with titles set in Adobe Garamond.

Printed in the United States of America on acid-free paper.

10 9 8 7 6 5 4 3 2 1

Portions of this book first appeared in the following publications, sometimes in slightly different form:

> *The And Review, The Beloit Poetry Journal, The Dominion Review, Kansas Quarterly, New Letters, Northeast, Perspective, Shenandoah*

"Angelita" won a *Kansas Quarterly* First Award for poetry, as well as a Seaton Award.

I wish to thank the National Endowment for the Arts and the Bush Foundation for their generous support during the completion of this book.

To see this book to its conclusion has taken decades longer than I anticipated. Along the way, many people were generous with their help and encouragement. In Italy: Tino and Mariapia Cirelli; Jay Michael Houlihan, and the Istituto Campano per la Storia della Resistenza; Luigi Compagnone; Fr. Giusto Pala; Roberto Cirelli; Franco and Gigliola Barbaresi; Maria Breda; Tullio Borelli; Nando and Fiorella Gabriele; and Cristina Cirelli. In the U.S., Abe Rothberg, Don Killian, Jay Mandt, and Paul Nevatt. Anyone who writes about Naples has to acknowledge a profound debt to the writings of William Sansom, Norman Lewis, Raleigh Trevelyan, Dominick Graham and Shelford Bidwell, and Farley Mowatt, to name a few. Nor should I leave out Vittorio Paliotti, Aldo de Jaco, Luciano de Crescenzo, and the quixotic, gifted, and frequently unlikable Curzio Malaparte. To them and many others, I make grateful acknowledgment.

This book is in loving memory of Tina.

Contents

A Word — xi

ONE: 1943
The Invasion	5
Nightingales	8
A War Pastoral	9
The Stonk	10
Bombs	12
Final Examination	14
Angelita	16

TWO: 1944
Wisteria	27
Landscape With Food	28
The Road to Benevento	29
Captain Diver's Dinner	30
Hunger	36
The Patron Saint	38
The Examination	41
Black Market	46

THREE: 1945
The Kingdom of Hands	55
The Wheel	57
The Patron Saint	58
The Neighborhood Clairvoyant	62
Old Clothes	64
The Market at Porta Capuana	67
Eating an Eel	68
Grandfather's Tale	70

About the Author — 77

A WORD

about the poems in this book. A half a century ago, William Sansom wrote that Naples was the only city in the world which under the very best conditions suffered from "both vertical and horizontal leprosy." "See Naples and cry," he wrote, "for the graft of rags and poverty, the old faces on the young—for the old city that is a bucket of filth, faith, tremendous life and hopelessness." That was the city which Allied troops entered on October 1, 1943.

To do so, the Allies had mounted a massive invasion at Salerno and Paestum three weeks before. But strong German resistance made the landing difficult, and even though the American commander General Mark Clark put a good face on it afterward, winning the way from the beachhead into Naples was costly and uncertain. It was only after heavy bombing and bitter fighting climaxed by a four-day insurrection mounted by the people of Naples themselves that the city fell. It was the first major European city to be liberated during the Second World War.

This collection of poems is about that liberation. There is no pretense at completeness. Rather, it is an anatomy of images. There is no single voice, but voices. There is no single style. But over all there is the compelling and paradoxical spirit of Naples itself, the old city whose people are full of both tremendous life and hopelessness.

—*Bruce Cutler*

Seeing the Darkness

Metropolis of a ruined Paradise
Long lost, late won, and yet but half regained!

.....

—Shelley, *Ode to Naples*

—ONE—

1943

...A war, even the most victorious,
is a national misfortune.

—Helmuth von Moltke, *Letters*

THE INVASION

Red Beach, Paestum

We began with a thing we would never see again.
The way we were, it never occurred to us
to see it as we should. There they were, the mountains of Cilento,
clear and brown and gathering shadows in their folds,
red-tiled roofs, the flash of whitewashed walls,
little heliclines of smoke in the middle distance
and the gray and grainy thorax of a beach spread out
horizon to horizon. And twenty yards from water's
edge, a stand of pine, its floor strewn thick
and dark with a hundred falls of cones and needles.

So we began with a thing that we'd never see again.
And the way we were, what we thought was now behind us—
a sea so thronged with ships they seemed uncountable,
Red Beach, LSTs, grids of wire mesh
floating our bogeys across the trap of sand—all that
would come again. Not knowing X-ray Beach at Anzio
was twenty weeks away. Or nine months beyond, D-day.
For us there was just one fact: ours were the wheels
that turned the shaft of Axis power toward defeat,
ours the ring of steel that would bring it to the ground.

*What one knows and doesn't know. Yesterday, we signed
an armistice with Italy. Today, we invade that Italy.
So much for intelligence. Reports? Not a single
sentence; all those agents, not a word. Mussolini?
Alive, dead. Here, there. No one knows.
The Germans? Somewhere. The greatest operation history
has seen, and no one knows a thing. And yet
one knows: those bodies all laid out like logs,
arm-by-arm, as if to stand inspection, the first assault,
and behind them, stockpiles not of shells
or food or medicine, but adding machines, typewriters, desks*

and chairs, as if some corporation gone massively astray
was floating in on waves from the standing ships.

What one knows and doesn't know... Beyond the sentries
we hear a muttering of voices **Panzerwagen Kriegsflotte**
or is it **pranzo ricotta** and in the ears of soldiers
fresh from Oconomowoc and Junction City, passwords
fly like swallows, in and out, in and out, until no one
can tell what's the name the name of this place
what's the way you say P-a e-s t-u-m?

You are here you are going forward your helmet angles off
a tree limb you wish this stand of pine was somewhere
down in Arkansas that you were too that what hits you
hadn't been so quick in coming that it was in some other life
but you're here you're standing still and it's moving
past you its face is not the face you'd dreamed of
but somehow brighter straighter greener soundless
and the wind? the dust? the rain? the enemy?
nothing: it's the thud of your boots on this piney floor
and the grunts are your grunts you are the thud, the grunt

You are here you are going forward but now the trees
are myrtles cypress laurels that green and gray
an olive tree Here's a pile of stones an opening the cool
celeste is sky, shell-like, with a shaft
of clouds as round and iridescent as a brace of pearls

Then rising up you see the ruins of the three great temples
their sandstone salmon-colored in the sun's last rays
shadows darkening their sculptured frieze their columns
fluting **aaeeiioouu** comes in a breeze comes
as you stop as you stand as you stare and again it comes

and you've begun with a thing you will never see again:
two wars,
 the first, frozen in stone, metope by metope,
where the Letoides raise their bows and Hercules grabs

Alcyoneus by the hair and runs him through. Where Ajax,
bending down as if to puke, runs his belly on his sword
and Hercules carries off the bodies of the Cercopes like milk cans
on a pole, their peckers dangling down.
                                        And the second,
crackling with small-arms fire, here, and now.

The eye of Clytemnestra, caught with ax in hand,
glints with a flake of ruby quartz against the setting sun.
And now you have it. We are the ones, the invaders,
we, dear reader, and around us yet another
book is being written, book around book,
whose author is more than a maker of names
and I never more than his eye and hand. And the thing
not one of us could have conceived—
the place that was only a name, and the end
of all our dying—Naples, was now just over the horizon,
across the mountains, around the bay, under
the volcano. There. Having begun with the thing we would never
see again, we fought our way out of it, and into the other.

NIGHTINGALES

A gray and greasy smoke screen
infiltrates the wood.
We have never seen
the camouflage so good,

barrage balloons so thick.
The 88s and small
arms fire have stopped. A quick
reconnaissance, all

is well. And now, night.
At ten, our two-inch mortars
bark, the moon comes up. Its light
falls like a rain of quarters,

makes aureoles
of laurel leaves. And caught
in the argent, gray-green, gold,
a nightingale, who ought

to be a casualty,
proclaims his ease. His ease!
A bird who has no right to be
is singing in these shredded trees.

We are bird-happy. And then
from a ridge the song resounds
ten times ten times ten
resounds resounds resounds resounds

A WAR PASTORAL

When they came, they came like honey from a jar,
spilling down the hillside in lazy swirls
and eddies. And all the bleating—it was as if
a raspy choir of the deaf was warming
up. Bobbing and baa-ing they came
over the banks of a gully, through a copse.
There must have been a thousand in the flock,
and you could see their fleece, hanging down
in heavy locks, and feel the little
thud of their legs, their shanks, their hocks

when fifty feet short of the road they began
to trip the mines. In that instant you would have thought
they were running over hummocks, tens
of them rising hip-high off the ground.
Then the ground began to shake, and it was blood
in the air, blood and wool and bone
and the rising screams of what once were sheep
careening off their fellows' flanks in front, behind,
driven, we could see now, by infantry, stalking
like shadows in the flaring, bloody sun.

THE STONK

your stonk is your American way of winning your war
your stonk is when you take your whole production, Rock Island
Arsenal '42, or whatever arsenal
in South Carolina, South Dakota, no difference
you throw it at the krauts from six to eight a.m.
maybe add a naval stonk to your stonk, being the really
big suckers that take out the little towns on the mountainsides
anyhow you stonk, you stonk the shit out of them

never go at them just at dawn just
with bayonets rifles and surprise like the Russians
never get drawn in because you get fucked I mean
really fucked by the flamethrowers, the British did,
just stonk them, stonk with mortars, stonk with anything you got
and keep on stonking, when you got no more stonk to stonk with
then send in tanks and infantry

when they do it from seven thousand feet your British air force
call it carpet bombing, your American word for it is stonk,
you will not remember carpet bombing, you will remember stonk
you will remember when it goes out because there is so much noise
your head is blown like inside out, your nose bleeds, your feet
ache, and you will never forget when it comes back at you

if you live to think about it
your stonk is to avoid casualties, promote battlefield efficiency
your stonk does pretty good except when the krauts have dug
   themselves in
deep and your stonk it really doesn't fuck them much and after a
   while
you get drawn in and you get fucked I mean really fucked by the
   flamethrowers

then you get stonked
and when you get stonked you get cold, when you get stonked you
   get the shakes
then you feel the heat from shrapnel smelling hot human
shit, that smell meaning someone's getting it, stomach wounds

blue flower by a shell crater, growing, not a violet
head wounds, leg wounds, chest wounds, or is it worse at sundown
the quiet, waiting, wondering who will get it, bad

cut your wrist, drive a needle in your ear
shoot your foot, cut the tendon in your heel

your stonk being your American way of doing war

BOMBS

How did I know? It was my window. Not the way you think, though.
Not from looking through the glass. I never saw one
that way. No one ever saw them that way. No,
I saw the sound. It was this way. I would be cutting carrots
and celery and tomatoes for the soup, you know, in little wedges
so they cook the better and take the oil just so, when I would
feel my knuckles. Feel, meaning I knew that they were there, the cold
of the water, or the heft of the knife, whatever. My knuckles,
and then, just the slightest z-z-z, z-z-z. Slighter
than the slightest of mosquito z-z-z, and I would look around,
but there was no mosquito, no fly, no bee in the bean flowers
on the balcony, no greedy beetle in the garbage pail. But the window,
yes, the window—the glass rattling ever so lightly
start, stop, start. And I would look into the street where the sun
so rarely shines: there's a little slash of light along
the wall across the way, and behind and above, a wedge of sky.
   "Your piece
of Naples," my Simonetta says. Nothing in it. Serene, untroubled,
   color of a shell
on a sunny beach. Then another z-z-z, and louder. And a dancing
   windowpane.
I could see it trembling, and I knew that somewhere near us now were
   bombers.
Not the Germans. Americans, and their planes were coming over
   Angri,
over Portici, sweeping low along the water, riding high
above Vesuvius, filling the sky with something we had never seen,
had never dreamed: the cloud that stopped the sun from shining,
stopped the wind from blowing, stopped your ears from hearing,
stopped your lungs from breathing, stopped your legs from running
and your arms from carrying, stopped your heart your blood your life
your hope your scream. Stopped everything. Everything. Still.

FINAL EXAMINATION

He's lucky.

He's a young partisan who has been captured, not by the German SS, who have just arrived at the outskirts of Naples, but by the Fascist police.

He undergoes the usual beatings. The police commissioner holds an adjunct professorship in the university law school, and after a few hours, hearing that the young partisan is a university student, he steps in and personally takes over the interrogation. After three days of questioning, the young partisan still remains silent, so the police commissioner makes him an offer. He tells him that this will be his "final examination." To complete it, he must choose between two alternatives. One: if he betrays the hiding places of his comrades, he will be sentenced to death. But the sentence will not be carried out; he will live, and eventually have his freedom. If the young partisan chooses this alternative, the police commissioner promises to plant false documents in the files proving that the information came from other sources. In this way, his reputation will remain untarnished, and in an anti-fascist victory, he will be in line for all the honors due a hero of the resistance.

On the other hand, if the young partisan refuses to give him the information about his comrades, the police commissioner tells him he is confident that in a few days, as a result of the terror caused by the arrival of the German SS, all his comrades will be rounded up. After which, they will be shot. Then the commissioner will plant "proof" that it was information from him which had betrayed his comrades and thereafter everyone will look upon him as a traitor and spit on his grave.

It is for him to choose. Which will it be? The young partisan asks for a day to consider, and goes back to his cell.

Sixteen hours later, he hangs himself.

ANGELITA

She came from behind, from behind their lines,
came out of the tall grass and the free-fire zone,
or rather her cries did, those sobs that seemed
to draw her to him through that dream of death,
following a flag of white breath and tears.

And he was digging. And the snick-snicking
of his spade seemed soothing when the German shelling
from the mountains suddenly ripped around him,
concussion rings and smoke and howls
behind the heaving earth in shellbursts.

He saw her. Six, with black and curly
hair, a torn and dirty dress.
And she saw him by his pile of dirt
and gear, his glasses glinting in the sun.
And when she did, she turned and screamed

then started to run straight at a mine field
by the road. And he jumped up and shouted "No!"
and she ran faster, so he dropped his spade
and grabbed his rifle, why, he never
knew, running after her and yelling "No!"

as she screamed "Mamma! Mamma!"
the two of them like Mutt and Jeff, racing
in a dead heat for the road where the one would put
her foot an inch too close and blow
them both right off this page until

he got her by the hair and neck, lifted
her off the earth, and underarm, like a doll
a fish   a bag of oats   he brought
her back to where? Not to the trench
or where she'd come from, not to the road

or the beach or the landing craft. To BHQ.
Where they propped her up on an empty ammo
crate beside the radio, gave her
a Hershey's, and made like apes, like apes at her:
"Me Joe. Who you?"

until they got to shouting, trying
to pry a name out of her. And she, sitting
there, eyes like a cat's, letting
each bite of Hershey's melt
on her tongue before she slowly swallowed.

How could she sit and eat that way,
he wondered. Someone hungry, like her.
More like a cat than he had thought.
Wide-set eyes and little ears.
A dark brown mole, below her hairline,

that moved. A mole, moving? From the edge
of her eyes across the smooth
skin of her forehead, moving. Into her hair.
And as he looked, she looked at him and saw
him watching what she felt. No longer was he looking

at her. Now his eyes were watching
something on her. And she began to cry.
Humiliation starts when someone's more
upset about a louse than you.
You become the thing, the louse.

So he went and brought a blanket and some odds
and ends of dago uniforms from a truck
upended at the mine field, and when he laid his hands
on her the second time, it was to strip her
of her dress. She struggled. He enjoyed it, now.

She was sticks. Joints and skin and sticks.
And dressed, she was a comic doll. A midget
Eyetie officer. All her lice
were buried in a rag bag of khaki wool
seven sizes oversize.

He held her dress to chuck it in the stove.
There was a fraying name tag sewn
inside its seam. "Angelita," a Spanish
name. He said it, and she bounded
off her box and ran to him as if

he'd pulled a string. The power of name.
He had her, now. But what he didn't know
was how she had him, too. How the thing
that's yours so perfectly becomes the thing
you'll never be without. Never. His Angelita.

* * * * *

It came from behind. From behind their lines,
his and Angelita's, the shelling now
incoming from the sea, the sixteen-inch
battleship big ones that took out tiers
of houses on the mountainsides

if they hit the mark, and juiced the vineyards
when they didn't. It didn't matter. Nothing
mattered in a stonk. Only that he was here
and there, one trench to another. And she
was his khaki shadow, playing store with ammo

crates and empty shell casings. And singing!
So busy and meticulous, and her song one long
invention. "Get rid of her," they told him. And he tried
to leave her in a barn with other refugees.
They wouldn't have her. She wouldn't stay.

So they went for the next few days, Capaccio
to Albanella Station, back
toward Battipaglia, one position
to another. The Germans hung in tough
and bludgeoned them with tanks and 88s

and nights, along the sea, you couldn't
tell just where the shells were coming from,
whose they might have been. The beach
lit up in giant flaming eels
and phosphorous anemones

when the ammo dumps went up, and the earth
and air together heaved and shook.
By day, an eerie calm of orchards,
the ripe and glowing fruit just out
of reach. And the olive groves, their leaves

gray-green and willowy and still.
And locusts popping up between
his boots, but brilliant blue. Blue?
Blue as a bay or a sapphire, and she caught them
in her hands and let them hum their way out

between her fingers into air, free
and blue ascending into free and blue.
They were near the railroad tracks. The lull
had seemed to draw deserters out
from clumps of trees. They walked the ties,

Italians, by the hundreds, waving and shouting,
showing themselves so freely. And why
so happy? Singing "Figli di nessuno,"
"Bella ciao." The only happy
noises in the country. And they teased the girl

and one began to cry when she reached
some cheese from a K-ration kit
abandoned for its candy and gave it up to him.
"Cient' anni!" "May you live a hundred years!"
he said it over "Cient' anni!"

She was looking at his boots. The sides
were torn and hanging and he'd tied some cords
around them. The toes and soles had separated
into a pair of empty mouths, lolling
at the bottoms of his pantslegs. But there was something,

blood-red, oozing. And Angelita cried out
"A-i-i" and knelt and put her fingers
in the flow and held them up. And the one
just shook his head, repeating
"Cient' anni!" "A hundred years!"

then plunged his right hand deep inside
his filthy coat, rummaged a moment
finding something hidden there,
and pulled it out, a red and shiny
strip of fabric—damask? taffeta?—

tore off a scrap and handed it to her
saying something as he did about the Madonna of Pompeii
protecting her. Protecting her! And afterwards
went off, limping down the tracks
again. And she turned away from the one

departing and handed up the scrap,
shaking her head, no, she didn't
want it. It was his. And he, who'd watched
the scene in silence, stuck it in his helmet
netting like a badge, laughing at them both.

* * * * *

What came, now came from behind both lines:
the shelling, Focke-Wulfs, P-38s
and Spitfires, Tiger tanks and Shermans,
mortars, mines, and panic. He saw it
coming. It was the fear of Germans

and a war that wouldn't go away,
their way, or any way.
Trigger-happy sentries. Platoons,
battalions, firing on each other.
Officers pulling out, abandoning

their men. And when the rumor flashed out *gas*
he panicked like the rest. But when she handed up
his mask to him it suddenly seemed
so foolish. A kind of costume for a play.
A child's mask. So he let it fall instead

down over her head, and she began
to shake beneath it with a kind of sob
of fear, or maybe mirth, he couldn't tell.
Whatever it was, she looked like a midget
elephant. Or monster mouse. And made

him laugh again. What followed then
was the kind of night a man might dream
about, two decades hence, when stillness
would spread out like dark enhancing velvet
around the diamond of that dream of death—

German gutturals of mortar fire,
the *whump* of Moaning Minnies, howl
of APCs and tanks in lowest gear,
the snap and scream of high-velocity shells
and chain-saw rip of automatic weapons

and over all, the sick fluorescence
of phosphorous flares and stench of cordite.
And just at dawn the naval batteries
began to take out city blocks
of landscape. But their shells were falling short

and the panic came again, and it came worse.
It was then a jeep appeared, improbable as a hiccup.
He didn't think, he only knew that when he saw
a pair of nurses riding on the back
he picked up Angelita, shoved her in-between them.

Terrified, all three. The driver yelled
and pointed. A carrier in flames had blocked
the road, so he turned and ran ahead.
He would remember, Angelita had been crying
but now she stopped. It was as if he heard

her silence. When his ears were set to split
it was as if he could hear her stillness, the breath
of her, singing. When he turned he saw a light
around the jeep and then he heard the last
tremendous *swoosh* and stomach-churning

crump as he dove down flat. When he got up
the bodies of the nurses hung like duffel bags
across the tailgate. And the driver knelt
in the middle of the road, still holding
the steering wheel, and slowly

started bending backward from the waist.
With a quiet gush his guts began to spill
across his legs as his body broke in half.
He found her in the jeep. Motionless.
A mound of olive drab. A pair

of outsize boots. He rolled her over.
Her face was pale and calm. A line
of blood was oozing back along the trail
the louse had blazed. Shrapnel. Little
more than a sliver. But the sliver had been enough

and she was dead. And the other bodies there
were dead. And the mountains seemed to gleam
with death. Those towns and vineyards, beaches,
orchards, all were slick and gleaming
with her death. He closed his eyes and screamed

and it was as if he pried the silence open
and something came from behind, from behind them all,
like a flame, like an arm, coming out of the air.
And it seized them and froze them in the splendor of its light.
And on his head her badge was glowing like a coal.

—TWO—

1944

There are so many hungry people that God cannot appear to them except in the form of bread.

—Corita Kent, *Enriched Bread*

WISTERIA

As he went to sleep it seemed to hug the wall and windows all
    the closer
its froth of purple flowers tiny lanterns in moonlight
the lacy racemes and leaves so sweet and feathery

in the big bed with his three brothers lying head by toe
four heads of broccoli in a box
four mackerel dreaming the stillness of water
four gulls with wings fixed on the azimuth of night

the chatter of small arms fire coming from the Vomero, screams
    of trucks
in their lowest gear, a howl out of a blind alley half a block away

and that vine as thick as a man's arm, rising to the second to
the third story and beyond
and the house a schooner on the tide riding steady beneath its mast

his bed a fabulous gondola sliding under a darkened bridge
in a fine warm sweet-smelling midnight summer rain

LANDSCAPE, WITH FOOD

The dump runs down a wide ravine
swelling, filling with the flow
of cans and crates. Holding an obscene
rawhide whip, a Negro

MP stands his guard. At the gate,
a crowd is gathering. He cracks
it, yelling *no! no!* at the late
arrivals. But then a truck backs

in, they all lunge past him. He
takes a can of gasoline
down the slope to set a sea
of fires and burn up every bean

in every can. It's not enough,
the barbed wire couldn't hold them back,
the blacksnake whip, the flaming stuff
they must not eat, nothing holds them back

and standing in that stinking stream
of spam, potato peels, pickles, cream,
grease, they eat. They eat it all.
Hip deep in flames, they eat it all.

THE ROAD TO BENEVENTO

The road to Benevento seems to flow
canal-like under fallow, falling leaves
of ash groves, around cutbacks piled with snow
and stone, then disappears in ragged sleeves
of tunnels. Halfway up a peasant sets
his snares, oblivious to November cold,
to graying thistles set like bayonets
and time that tightens in the dead leaf-mold
driving down the worm. No one else is near.
No light or voice or music makes the still-life
more than mortal. No hope, no fear
deceives him into thought. The shape of life
runs steel-engraved within, like second sight
of ages more dark and cold, and longer night.

CAPTAIN DIVER'S DINNER

Enter a waiter, flitting between the tables
with a platter. "Signò'—guardat' a stu bellu
pesc'!"—sweeping it underneath our noses
like a limp white Stuka. Elegant
head, bluish eye, the gills just
pink and red, the spine and flesh
garnished with sprigs of parsley, gobs

of melon. So much show. Fish fanciers
would know this body doesn't match its head
any more than frog's legs would a chicken.
A little shark is not a sea-bass. First
they cut it into portions, arrange
it so, garnish, then dive-bomb the customer
with what he'll think he'll see. But even

getting here was like that—the tenements
collapsed, heaps of rubble looming
taller than our half-tracks, a smell ranker
than sewer-slime infiltrating the air. The busy
lines of flies made mad by it. And then
the cripples, the deformed, buzzing too,
hunchbacks offering up their lucky

humps to anyone who'll buy a lottery
ticket, cretins with enormous heads
bobbing like boiling onions, propped
up against the ruins of a wall. A dwarf,
hustling cut-price coffins. Whores.
And then those others, sweeping down on you, offering
five and six year-olds to do

your pleasure. You've come a long way from New Haven.
And it wasn't just the ocean voyage,
it's as if you fell five hundred years
downward in time—back to Boccaccio,
the plague raging, a Court of Funereal
Miracles about to form. It was here in Naples
Fiammetta burned into Boccaccio's eye

in the Church of San Lorenzo. And more. In San Domenico
Maggiore, the founder of theology was lessoned
by its crucifix. And not far off, the ages
and cycles of history came inching into nearness
for Giambattista Vico. All these places, rubble
now. And the elegance of Sannazzaro's fishermen
reduced to this illusion. Dogfish fillets.

My night on the town. And Mendelson, the rabbi,
along. What to say. Cold. A brazier
set in the corner, belching disinfectant.
And the customers—doctors, lawyers, millers—
"Machers," Mendelson chimed in—huddled
around the tables, wrapped in overcoats.
A study in olive drab, those coats

sewn up from stolen GI blankets,
cut and tailored as if for opening night
of a Marlene Dietrich movie. Turnips
for vegetables, the wine resinous. Bread
fit for the wood pile. But they sat
with forks in hand, dreaming meals
and talking food and waiting for their plates.

That, too. Medieval. Separating out
a moment from what's around it with such
"Worldly lust," Mendelson chimed in again. And called up
Saul of Tarsus to mind. But it was then
some beggar boys, *scugnizzi,* came sidling
through the door. No one seemed to see them.
They moved like ragged afterthoughts among us

waiting for the slightest show of your indifference
before impaling with their eyes. That second
was their please-and-thank-you. A grubby hand
flashed out, your leftovers were gone. Disappeared.
I marveled at it. No one took offense
or shoved them off. We were communing
with our food, and they were merely the world.

It was barbarous. We nursed our wine,
the waiter came to show dessert.
It was a kind of marzipan concocted out of stolen
Allied sugar, shaped to look
like wan and greasy filberts, pistachios,
acorns. Then came coffee ground from chicory,
served so sweet you hardly knew.

And so we talked of Fichte, and how idealism
can never be a mode of thought.
Merely a speculative point of view.
It was something comforting, our try at making
German idealism intelligible, asserting
our selves in the invocation of the Absolute I

when the beggar boys came back. And wheeled
inside a spidery cripple, staked face-
down on a kind of skateboard, and while
the piles of rags that were his limbs
twitched and his mouth stammered at the filthy
floor, the boys this time made
off with half a loaf of bread

jamming it between his teeth, silencing him.
Even the arrant thievery of that loaf
distracted no one from our food or the yammer
of our conversations. And just as quickly as the boys
appeared, they dragged him out again,
skate wheels clicking like a tiny train
across the tiles of the sidewalk out in front.

The tic-tic of his going barely faded
when the doorway filled with half a dozen
oval faces, moonlike in stark
black uniforms, black boots, black stockings,
black hair cut short like prisoners. Weeping,
the girls stood hand in hand until it seemed
that someone pushed them forward toward us.

Why us? I remember thinking as the first
of them collided with a fat man in a chair
and the girls began to wail and pull
at one another, their eyelids fluttering,
and you could see the pinkish membranes
underneath. "Dear God, they're blind,"
I said to Mendelson, who sat transfixed

as one let go of the other and they groped
their ways among us. It was as if some other
hand directed her to turn and feel
her way our way, that girl who was young
enough to be my daughter, her dry
and parchment skin, cheeks hollowed by the winds
of hunger, two lines of sorrow running

from beside her nose below the corners of her mouth,
the tiny muscles at the bridge of her nose
and in-between her eyebrows knotted with weeping.
She turned her visage toward me. I saw
her lips were trembling, and it seemed the tears
were welling from the sightless center of her soul.
Her nose had told her "Here is food"

and following that dark induction toward us,
arms and hands extended, palms
downward, fingers rigid, it was as if
she did in some way see. And so she came
before me. I could see the whiteness
of her teeth accede to something gray,
lips to cracks and fever blisters,

and something more—there was a ribbon
struggling through her close-cropped shocks of hair,
a rag with what was once a fleur-de-lis
knotted at the crown by someone's hand.
Just for a second, I could see her coming
from the shadows of the Church of San Lorenzo,
her face burning like a flambeau in my eyes

before the cantilenas of her hunger turned
to howls, and it was 1944 again. Mendelson
pushed my arm. The plate with crumbs
of marzipan. I filled a spoon and put
it just between her lips. She stopped,
closed them around the spoon, licked it off,
then raised her arms and hands in unison

to thank me. As she turned away, forks
and spoons flashed out, the orphans' open
mouths were filled, one from this side,
one from that. But no one seemed
to see anything. And when it ended, the girls
went groping out the door. Our meal
went on. Whatever it was, was over.

The edges of a darkness seemed to draw
around me, and I shuddered. Yet I didn't lose
my calm. I heard no voices. There was only
a kind of ringing emptiness, an inwardness,
a pregnancy of silence
demanding something. I could only stammer
"What are we supposed to do?"

as my comrade sat there, stricken. And I thought,
those girls were weeping when they came and weeping
when they left. Even beyond the prison of their blindness
this war had sentenced them to... To what? I knew
that none of us could ever come to terms with that.
I knew we had no way to come to terms.
Seeing their darkness was all that we would see.

HUNGER

The bay as smooth as aspic. Hulks
of frigates, merchantmen, LSTs and tenders
listing as if at ease. As if reclining

in the water. There are bands of women
scraping limpets off the rocks,
scraping for a faintly fishy something

for a broth; there's nothing now to eat
except a rocky broth of limpets.
Sea slugs. Barnacles and whelks.

* * *

You miss the coffee, the little symphony
of oils and aromatics performing at your corner
bar. Your morning serenade, espresso,

a nice toccata, cappuccino, something
presto, anisette. And it's not just the coffee,
it's the friends, friends who were more your friends

for flirting with the girl cashier, laying
bets on the Sunday games. Talking,
taking it all in. All you can remember. Coffee.

* * *

There are no pigeons, there are no cats.
No frogs. No dogs. Every night you sleep
in peace. You listen to the walls settle.

Today there was a tiny plate
of chicken maw set out beside
a head whose beak was neatly trimmed.

A single calf's foot. A lovely chunk
of windpipe. And the butcher's ice-blue eyes,
gazing out through clean, cracked glass.

THE PATRON SAINT

On May 6, 1944, a reliquary containing the blood of San Gennaro was elevated by the Bishop of Naples. For the first time in decades a miracle failed to occur and the blood did not liquefy. The people believed that it was the saint's response to a crowd of British and American troops who had come to jeer at the ceremony.

Conquerors, I am alive in this reliquary! I am the owner of my blood! I am Saint Januarius, and Naples is my city!

Yes, I am quite aware that in the past three hundred years my people have ceased to call me by my Latin name. They call me San Gennaro now, and in the future they may call me something else, but I shall be always be here, no matter what name they use!

The earliest representation of me is an icon which shows me with two faces. It represents the first miracle connected with my birth: I was born with the ability to look two ways—into the past and into the future. Some of you today are making unkind interpretations of my two faces. Little do you know how heavy has been the burden of being able to see the past and the future in the present moment.

Every patron saint specializes in gestures of service to his people, sometimes small, sometimes large. As for me, epitaphs are one of my small specialties. With this war there have been so many dead and so many epitaphs to inspire in the minds of my followers! Now I shall let you in on a secret. While each epitaph I inspire may sound different to your ears, in reality they all stem from a single one, my Ur-epitaph:

> *Your life did not last sixty years, I think.*
> *In the long insomnia of time, a wink.*

Before you, eons, when you did not exist.
Ahead, eternity. You will not be missed.

"Epitaph?" I hear you saying, "you call that an epitaph? What kind of a saint would put ideas like that into someone's head?" Let me explain. All I can do for the dead, yes, even down to inspiring their epitaphs, has nothing at all to do with the dead themselves. They are, after all, dead. Instead, what I do is meant for the living. "Yes," you scoff, "and these wretched people are the living. Just look at them."

"But they are the lucky few—" I say. And you interrupt again, "Lucky? But in what way? How are they lucky to have to live with no water and no food in the bombed-out ruins of this city?"

Patiently I reply, "Yes. They are lucky. A living person, anyone at all in my city who has survived down to today, is an exception to the rule." You ask, "And what rule is that?" and I say, "It is the rule that in Naples from its earliest days as a Greek colony, the dead have always outnumbered the living, and forever will do so. Through war, famine, earthquake and pestilence, three have died for every man or woman who survives, year after year, century after century. Don't you see—that is why the living are lucky. And they need a continual reminder, and not just a reminder, an exhortation, about their condition."

Ah, you do not answer. Perhaps now you begin to see that unlike other patron saints who are mere minions, doing small favors for their followers, I have been given a far more difficult and demanding task. My great goal, the one that makes my presence unique among all the saints, is something my followers may suspect but will never know for sure, so I shall tell you these next things in confidence, and you will understand why.

I am the patron saint of the real.

My followers will never lack for the blessing of the knowledge of the way things are. Their lives will never wander off into foolish galaxies of thought and emotion where life turns its face away from them and as a result they become incapable of survival.

I am their intuition of the inevitable.

Through me they will learn to be strong. There is muscle in my counsel. It links the flesh of their desires with the bone of what is. I teach a faith that is older than the present faith, for I myself am older than the garments of the religion they have clothed me in.

Yes, scoff all you like today. But I will continue to look into the past and the future as my people live in each moment, day after day, decade after decade, millennium after millennium, and I will proclaim that they should believe in me and I will continue to serve them in my special way.

I am the harbinger of what can never not be.

THE EXAMINATION

He was not a hunchback. So inherently no luck in him.
But famous, yes. The smallest of the small.
"Look up!" you'd say, to get someone's attention,
but from him-to-us the world was always up,
nowhere but. His hands so dexterous, so
diminutive, they'd fit inside a woman's
pelvic cavity, finger her ligatures and scars,
zero in a speculum or swab exactly
on a canker. He was Doctor Pollici. And when the MPs pushed
the first half-dozen women through the doors, there was a rush
of frigid air that caught the soldiers
at their knees and thighs, and him around his ears.
The women cried, clutching their drawers and coats
and shopping bags as orderlies pushed them
into chairs and locked their feet in stirrups.
Ab pudenda disce omnes and all
in a row *et labia* as he approached with his tiny stepladder.
He could see the knuckles, the little scabs
and scars, the rings hanging moon-like by his eyes.
Then the sighs, the handkerchiefs, the clink of coins...

*

Major O.D. Blade was AMG Staff
Surgeon, and he found this Doctor Pollici a pain
in the ass, first because he was a midget, a goddamn
midget, not to mention local, one
of those wop doctors who smells your piss and sets leeches
on your veins. Just saying it, a local midget, didn't
sound medical. Or military. Or anything he'd ever
heard of. Only in Naples could it be so weird.
There was Pollici, on his little stepladder, a mouse
sniffing cheese, his squeaky voice, "Va bene,"
and swabs as long as his forearm falling on a tray
the orderlies doubled over just to hold. And his fame,
for what? Plastic jobs, snip-and-stitching,
reconstructing hymens. Instant virgins
were Pollici's specialty, because in Naples... because
in Naples they were better even than original, they took
the local studs three nights to break. And because
in this city of studs, it was O.D. Blade who had to have
a major VD epidemic on his hands. And the best
that Naples had to offer was this goddamn local midget...

*

We're a stream of sheep, Teresa thought. About
to hustle through a dip. Or worse. There they'd been,
standing in a queue for bread, when a jeep pulled
up beside them, and all that shouting, pushing,
truncheons swinging, the women herded one
street to another. The Negro MPs frightened her
almost as much as the Moroccans—*les Goums du Generale
Juin*—and how was she to tell the difference?
Simonetta wouldn't stop her sobbing. And the crowds
by the hospital gate, the MPs pushing, pushing them,
o'sciaquapalle that red faced ball-
washer of an orderly shouting "Panties down
girlies, the Americani want a look at what you've got!"
And the sob, the moan, the shouts that broke out then.
Not even the Germans picked up housewives for a thing
like this. The orderlies took hold of them,
pushed them into chairs, rocked them backward, raised
their feet, threw back their skirts and spread their legs...

*

Moaning, sobbing, yelling, the noise became
a din, became a roar. From the first the women fought
the MPs and the orderlies, crying *mannaggia o' cazzo tuio
và' a fa'nculo a sòreta* but the orderlies pushed,
the MPs pulled, and the AMG VD
inspection lumbered like a bullfight
through the morning. Speculum, swab, smear,
he could tell with his nose. It was like a hundred different
kinds of codfish, but he could tell. Standing
on his stepladder, he could see the girl was virgin, imperfect
as nature made her. The mother held her hand
from the chair beside. She was clean. Speculum, swab,
it was all the same. "Va bene." Pollici turned
to Major Blade: "You see? a virgin, a real virgin,
still *in vivo*, can't you see?" Pointing with his swab.
And Blade had answered, "Fuck the virgins."
One hears his voice coming from above, easy with arrogance,
clean as the smell of their Lifebuoy soap.
Conquerors, they touch your skin, and suddenly your skin
becomes their single thought, their appetite, their dream.

*

But then something sudden, as if a huge invisible
bird had spread its wings across that chaos, had moved
the air, had thrown a second darkness over them, one
no one had ever dreamed of. And from just one
phrase: *mines! delayed action mines!*
And as if to show that the truth should come
by word of mouth and only later out of GHQ,
a courier arrived with orders: *threat of German DAMs
evacuate port area   1400 hours
all personnel, all civilians out.*
Blade had blanched. The fucking city was a bomb,
that's what it was, with a midget doctor for a fuse.
Pollici had paused, then clambered down from the warm
ramparts around his ears. He dropped his speculum and swab.
"Va bene," he began to say, but the women now were pulling
up their drawers and putting on their coats and shouting
fessi! as they started out the doors hanging now so limply
open, bleeding into the streets, their lingering cries
rising and redoubling in the rubble to a howl...

BLACK MARKET

In a shack, in a field of mud. That's where she is.

*

Before, in a building. On the ground floor, with a window.
And a door, how nice. A little moving wall to keep the in in

and the out out.

*

Then the bombers came. Over Angri, over Portici,
airplanes with two tails. With women driving them.
I know. By the wreckage of the one that fell, I found two
blondes. The bodies were not broken overmuch.
They were nude. They were marvelous to see.

Those teeth, glinting in sunlight.

*

Antò, my friends said, you ragpicker,
you junkman, you dummy, you just stood there and looked?

And yeah, they came out of the sky.
Airplanes with two tails, with women driving them.
Out of the sky, see?

*

After the bombing, Maddalena and I, we built this shack.
Broken beams. Pieces of tin. Old drapes and blankets.
A duet of airplane seats.

We were found by cats.

*

Radio said, Italians, resist the Germans.
Don't sell, don't work, don't give,
just take. Take the food, the tools, the wire,
the parts. Take anything from the Germans.

The junkman is the star of this show.

*

When the Americans came, the white soldiers painted
their faces with pomades the colors of earth,
of night.

      The black soldiers
didn't paint themselves, not with white or anything.
They sat for hours in the sun. When
they got up, they could speak our language
perfectly.

*

Then came the Moroccans. The Goums.
When they raped the mothers, they liked to have
the children watch. They liked
to make the mothers comfort them,
repeating how they'd saved them from the Germans.

Then they'd take one, and slowly cut its throat.

*

I hid my Maddalena.
Stay, stay in the shack, I said.

A cave of cats.

*

The firm of Antonio Quercia, a cart without a horse,
a frame without a mirror, a bed without a spring.
Rags without bones.

Lovely wire for telephones.
Pieces cut, and cut again. Resist-the-Germans pieces.
Little copper snakes. Scotched. Nesting in my cart.

*

Trade, trade, nothing to eat.
The Allies bring us
nothing. We never called
their market Black. We called it
American.

Money.

*

It began to rain.
Maddalena took a fever, then a cough.
Blood.

The cats' eyes, little moons.

*

We began to see these marvelous tins.
The British had them. Inside, not tomatoes, but sweet cakes, chocolate, marmalade.
Can you remember, marmalade...

There was a sergeant selling them.

Money.

*

From the Americans there were little grayish tablets.
They looked like chalk.
Swallow one, you won't go hungry for a week.
Your dick will grow.

*

Who will buy my rags?

*

American MPs.
They stopped me in the morning.
They took apart my cart.
They found my wire, they held it up.

Patriotic wire, I said.
Thieving bastard, the MPs said.

*

They shackled me.
I have to go to my house, I said.
My Maddalena!

You got no house, the MPs said.
Your house is Poggio Reale prison,

your house is seven years, on the inside.

*

You say the Allies won?
Good luck to you.

That wire was German.

*

It keeps on raining.

In a shack, in a field of mud. That's where she is.
The cats, gone.

*

Under a heap of rags
and beams and sodden
blankets

little rainbows
of excrement.

Not a sound.

—THREE—

1945

Our life is at all times and before anything else the consciousness of what we can do.

—Jose Ortega y Gasset, *The Revolt of the Masses*

THE KINGDOM OF HANDS

As you reach into your pocket, suddenly you touch an alien hand.
But wait: it's not a hand, it's a skittish five-legged animal
nosing through your bills, your small change, your pocket lint.
Then it's gone. Had you forgotten? This is Naples,
the Kingdom of Hands, where its tired and hungry subjects go
  wandering
off on their own to visit some of the warm and inviting places
in the human hemisphere. Like today, someone's hand
was having a short Easter vacation inside your coat pocket.
Tomorrow, someone else's will be laid out on the sandy beaches
of your hip pocket. Not that your cuff links or your scapular
wouldn't be welcome souvenirs, but those hands would just as soon
fold a ten thousand lire note so cunningly that the teller
will count it twice in a stack they are depositing at his window,
or pull off something magical—levitate the lid of a display case
in a pastry shop and cause one eggy rum-soaked cake to disappear,
or pull in society's clotheslines overhead and relieve them
of the oppressed laundry hanging out over the streets, those bedsheets
straining themselves into squares and weeping cold, gray tears.

A policeman is having his morning coffee in the bar downstairs
and when you tell him some of the sadder Tales of the Wandering
  Hands
his eyes fill with tears. He says that except for the tourists,
and killers who try not to leave their fingerprints behind,
and girls who get chilblains when February winds come off the sea,
the glovemakers really have it tough. Tough's not the word,
you say, all over town there are hands, hands, hands,
naked as the day they were born. They've got no shame, he says.
Shame's not the word, you interrupt, any time, day or night,
you can see them. They pat, they stroke, they tease, they grab,
  they let go,
they nip, they plunge... You pause while these images sink in.
He says they've noticed down at headquarters that some have
  gone over

to the province of the arts, recreating Roman deities, evoking
Etruscan burial necklaces. Indistinguishable from originals.
Creativity is good therapy, you say. Which reminds you—
has he noticed how the church by Fontanelle cemetery is filling up
with women's hands? It is? he echoes. *Is* is not the word, you say;
they're cleaning bones, laying them out, forming the initials of
  the dead
on tables in the ossuary. But more than that, does he know what
they're really doing? Working up an outline. An outline?
he asks. Yes. Next week, preliminary sketches; week after next,
  first drafts;
a volume is shaping up, something they can pray for, pray to, protect,
whatever. You say they're writing a *book?* he asks, puzzled. Well,
  not really
a book-book, you answer. Something more like a dictionary.
Or a speller. For words beginning with sounds no one has ever
  heard.

THE WHEEL

Outside, night. You can barely breathe.
There's a howl down at the end of the street, the blind end,
where the *goums* of Generale Juin are dancing
with daggers in their mouths. A mandolin is gutting
right along against their stream of Berber
curses. Around, above, in room
after room in blackness, babies, our little hopes,
cry, fall silent, cry, fall silent,
tentative as candles. Flickering, fading out.

The door of the convent of the Little Sisters
is lit, but signed OFF LIMITS. Those
who know say there are days when if you knock
you'll hear "What do you want?" You say, "One blessing,
Sister," and a door will open in the wall.
You can put your little hope inside
and the door closes and the wheel within
that wall will turn and suddenly your little
hope is gone. Gone to the other side.

Some of the girls come carrying their hopes
all the way back from the German labor
camps. Most of them get their hopes right here.
No matter. The wheel turns, their hopes go off,
they disappear. But you, you stand right here,
you want to know what happens to a hope.
"It's a mystery," the Sisters say, "it's not
to ask." But you aren't dancing, and you
don't want to dance. You want to know!

THE PATRON SAINT

Allied commanders ordered soldiers present during the elevation of the reliquary of San Gennaro in 1945 to observe absolute silence. For the first 45 minutes the blood of the saint remained solid. Then a mysterious voice called out for the troops to stand at attention. In the fiftieth minute the saint's blood liquefied, to the great joy of the people.

Conquerors, you have heard my voice! You have shown me respect. Now I can confide in you. Listen well.

First: note that all around you, my people are crying for joy. But mark me, in a few hours they will again be crying out that they are suffering. "Why do we have to suffer?" they will ask, and again, I will answer them: "Of course you are suffering, and you will continue to suffer. It is because you have been favored. Don't you remember? Have you forgotten my words already?" Predictably they will have forgotten, and predictably, they will go on beseeching me. And they will begin to feel tormented because they want an answer and can't get one—just as I told them!

There is more. At the same time they feel their suffering they will be surprised to find another and quite unexpectedly different condition setting in. What is it? Boredom. Yes, boredom! Why? Why, indeed! It is paradoxical, absurd. They haven't a clue, and no one can tell them why, or what to do about it.

So again they will come to me for an answer. I shall say, "My people, this is my answer: *Yes!* Boredom is a thing! It is a thing in life, like the suffering of being one of the favored few! *Yes,* it happens!"

To no avail. My people will not be satisfied. The longer they feel tormented and bored and unsatisfied, the more they will come to suspect that their condition must be the result of some divine act. They think it must be God's judgment that boredom should run parallel with their suffering.

But if that is true, it is absurd! It is an indignity! Why must they feel such an indignity? They think it can only have come about because they don't count. In the scheme of things, they are nothing. And not just that—their very nothingness is another sign of that divine curse!

I see all this, and I understand. As war, poverty and disease have come in unending cycles, my people have been numbed. It is this numbness which has prompted them to feel they are the least important people on the face of the earth. They have felt something in their spirit begin to wither, and as time has gone on, that feeling has become both their deepest intuition and their deepest fear. It has persuaded them that there can never again come a time when they will feel important.

They cry out for a miracle! A real one! They want me to intervene, to turn events around for them. But along with this desire, three thousand years of living in this place have also taught them not to expect anything. They instinctively sense who I am and what I am and what I have always been, from the beginning:

> *I am the patron saint of their real condition.*
> *I am their inspiration of the inevitable.*
> *I am the harbinger of what can never not be.*

My people are much too vital just to throw up their hands and die. The flesh of their desire is truly linked to the bone of what is, for mine is the muscle that joins the two. So with me they go on. How? They learn to wait. For over three thousand years they have learned better than any other people on earth how to wait. Food, music, street theater, spontaneous song, passion—especially passion—these they know well, and in passing the time with them they have also acquired a unique kind of vision.

They have come to see that they exist, not in one, but in two lives, and not in one, but in two cities. One life is the unfortunate one they must live in these crowded streets, day-to-day and week-to-week. The other life is the one they live by joining hands with their pastimes. When you say a Neapolitan lives for food, it is not a mere figure of speech. In the same way, my people have come to see that they live in two cities. One city is the one they live in, here, century after century. But there is a second one which lies beneath their feet, and they have learned to live there too. When you say Neapolitans are a people you are really speaking of a union of two peoples, and of the populations of two cities—the city of the living, and the city of the dead. Courtyard and graveyard. Neapolis and necropolis.

When you see my blood exposed as a relic in this church, it is not a dead thing. It is blood as capable of life as much as anyone else's. Like a hand it reaches out, it seeks to infuse the warm bodies of living human beings so as to help make it possible for them to live in this world. In the same way, every store, every church, every tenement on top of ground in this city stands on the ruins of three thousand years of its predecessors underground. A modern department store stands on the ruins of a Phoenician trading post. A government bureau squats on the foundations of a Greek temple. No matter how great the variety of buildings above ground, there is an even more exotic urban sprawl underground—a Hohenstaufen armory, an Angevin counting house, a Roman ship's outfitter. Whenever a new building soars into the air, its builders must dig. Whenever a new thing comes into existence, it must rest on the remains of an ancient ancestor.

There is an army of ancestors beneath your shoe soles, waiting for you to join hands with them. Call on them—they will reach out!

Visit the catacombs where I am buried. You will come down from the soaring walls of my church into a burial maze. In finding your way to my tomb, somewhere along the way you will turn a corner and stand in front of a column of travertine marble. It is about a meter in height, and twenty centimeters thick, with a cunning, rounded tip. Even the dullest person should comprehend, but if not, one of my faithful followers has inscribed that column with a single word:

Πρίαπος

Yes, my original name, revealed in this, my epitaph. My true name, written in the father of languages. I am buried with my priestesses, the priestesses of Priapos. I am your spiritual father. Reach out to me! Our hands will join forever, here in the city of the dead.

Your life will not last eighty years, I think.
In the long insomnia of time, a wink.
Before you, eons when you did not exist.
Ahead, eternity. You will not be missed.

THE NEIGHBORHOOD CLAIRVOYANT

Your body should respond to therapy.

Remember to receive a stranger with true hospitality.
A lover can be won only with difficulty.

The respect of others is the coin of envy.

Death alone can command the whole of your passion.

*

Your body is the coin of envy.
Your lover should respond to therapy.

A stranger alone can command the whole of your passion.
Remember to receive the respect of others with true hospitality.

Death can be won only with difficulty.

*

Remember to receive your body with true hospitality.

A lover alone can command the whole of your passion.
The respect of others should respond to therapy.

A stranger can be won only with difficulty.

Death is the coin of envy.

*

Your body commands the whole of your passion.
A stranger is the coin of envy.
The respect of others can be won only with difficulty.

Remember to receive your lover with true hospitality.

Death will respond to therapy.

*

Your body can be won only with difficulty.
The stranger will respond to therapy.

The respect of others alone can command the whole of your passion.
Your lover is the coin of envy.

Remember to receive death with true hospitality.

OLD CLOTHES

A couple hundred weeks, a couple kilos more or less
and there you are. You look at them, they look at you.
You're separated, not divorced. A seamstress down the street

comes in to let them out, but it's too late. It's Tuesday,
March fifteenth, she says any more your stuff won't move,
she might as well put on the cap and ring the bell,

it's her verdict, it's the end. You argue, but she's more than firm—
"Ma và, è scassà!" They're not just worn, they're busted, like the
    chair seat
or the mattress in the store room. It's time to shed a coat, two pairs
    of pants,

two shirts, not to mention one and one half pair of shoes,
the narrow pair your toes are jammed in like straphangers on a
    streetcar,
plus the one, the half whose lost left brother languishes

somewhere between your wardrobe and a confirmation dinner
—was it last December? Admit, these clothes are strangers to you,
they're not your friends, they don't protect your interests any more.

Out they go. To Salvatore the Soaper. Into the castoffs'
foreign legion in the bed of Sally's three-wheel moto
carryall, where they go to get inducted and their six-day basic
    training

back at Sally's Prone Pressure Method Clothes Reanimation
Center, where there are four complete revivings. First at the hands
of Sally's wife, Teresa, where the tears are mended, buttonholes
    restored,

burns repaired with snippets from the seams. Laundry next, with
    Sally's
daughter Filomena at the tubs, the disappearing act for armpit
moons, a greening-up for florals. Then second daughter

Angelina applies the iron; you'll never know
they ever hung on anything except a hanger. And here's one
last stop for the special cases, suedes and rabbit furs

that Sally comes by, the Wake Up Room, where he steams them
    back
from comatose to bushy. It's as if those skins had felt a sultry
sea-breeze, breathed it in, told themselves *hey*

wait a minute, let's shake our tails, let's go for broads and Bang
they're wide awake. He combs their hair, he hangs them on a rack
and Sally's carryall is full of home-delivered fashions.

But shoes are different. Sally farms them out.
There's nothing human about what's left of them, I mean their
    mouths
are hanging open, tongues are lolling, vamps all scarred

like boxing gloves. It's Sally's second cousin, Fat
Gennaro, that he badgers, that he dares to intervene, take out his
    tools
and do a transplant, here's a shank, here's an insole,

slip a counter from a brown shoe on the backstay of a black,
cut a sole and tack a heel and dye the whole bunch
black and blacker. And a pair of English oxfords rises

on the ruins of two boots. But there's always one, that half a pair,
waiting for its brother. Or at least a partner. Fat Gennaro
waits for February, things are slow, he improvises something

tale e quale. Presto, the second half, black and beautiful,
maybe the toe box or the cap a little canted, tanned
or textured three points off, but *there,* beside the other.

"They're just alike!" "Oh no, they're not!" "They're just alike!"
Back and forth, Fat Gennaro and the buyer argue
but Fat Gennaro has the clincher: "You think these shoes look
   different?

"They're standing still. Start to walk, they look the same,
I mean, what do shoes *do?* They walk, one ahead, one behind,
so who can tell they're not the same?" "And if you stop?"

the buyer presses. "You rest one foot on top of the other,
like I'm doing now. Act unconcerned. No one will know."
And that's how Fat Gennaro moves the shoes. I mean,

in Naples, if you look carefully, you'll see something of yourself
on everybody else—an English worsted you really liked,
those brogues that looked like cordovan—it's as if you've spread
   yourself

all over town. It's Sally's satisfaction, not to mention
Fat Gennaro's. Not to mention yours. You're on the skin.
You're warm, you're moving through the streets. It's dinner time.

THE MARKET AT PORTA CAPUANA

comes out of the ground, comes out
before sunrise with a *scric-scric*
of bicycles, *zump* of a handcart's iron
stumps, *ish* of willow baskets.
Little moons of breath break out
in the dying night air, *uffa*
the potatoes, *aouf* the tomatoes.

Your mattress is full of lumps. You know
the dark carnations are moving in. In the mouths
of shopfronts, squid spread out like soap lather.
A zoot suit hangs in public execution.
Voices argue, and they rise half way
to music. It is the moment when outraged
ostrich feathers are arrayed against the cheese

in bulbous bunkers, when zeppelins of watermelon
zero in on the pendent powers
of salami. When someone starts to sing,
a fifth floor window opens. Reparations,
restorations, rise in jugs
of wine and oil, pasta angel
hair, and very pure, egg-noodle, stars.

EATING AN EEL

He's not your everyday catch, your eel.
He doesn't think so, either. From the tip
of your net he's all whip and thrust, a kind
of slippery missile on its second phase,
then he's out of your hands and into the creel,
eighteen hundred grams of him, his mottled skin
slick as a piston as he flashes the feathery
aileron of his tail and zooms and flips
and tucks in maydays of evasive action
decoded on his microdot of brain
in out around through
arrive alive survive survive

He has eaten his way through at least two lives.
Spawned in the South Atlantic, he fingers
over its alps toward El Dorado,
and the Spaniards would take him then, as a chub
for supper-snacks, with lemon salt.
But the ocean yawns, the nets are thin,
other plans have made him. In a couple
of years, he's knocking around in pools
of sharks near Baltimore and New Orleans,
working his way upriver, taking
to fresh water like a retriever. You'd think
he was one of the Catfish-Sunfish gang

but in his heart there's a tiny tag that reads
thank god that i'm italian
and he's off again, sounding
in the wake of the SS Raffaello.
At Gibraltar, there's a welcome hint
of porpoises and camel-piss; farther
on, the squid and octopus
are inking in. Now it's the social amenities
that count—crowds of mullet, caravans

of tuna, greening parks of prawns,
plus the insistent *marsh and sun
and salt marsh and sun and salt*

and he's there, right in your net. Well,
not quite. There has to have been at least one
shudder in his white and tender flesh,
in the spreading of his jaws, in letting the slick
and slightly barleyed swampwater
sluice a thumb of anchovy in—in the shocks
that are the wonder of his skin which is both home
and habitat—at least one, you think, as you hold
him fast in yesterday's newspaper. Cut
his hissing head off. Gut him. Cut him
into little dancing sections. You see
how he's alive, in all his bones? He is your meat.

GRANDFATHER'S TALE

Start with what's in the blood. Old blood,
but your blood. Meaning old hungers, reaching out
through a maze of streets and alleyways
where there's always a waft of eels dancing
in boiling oil, and crusty loaves

of bread browning under domes of ovens,
whispering *savor*. And *remember*. The two
together, whose sum remembered comes to be
your hunger. All your life, your hunger.
Now add in the living: a father,

a mother, three daughters and a pair of sons.
Three times a day they ate, and yet
they were always hungry. They seemed to hear
that whisper. After meals, they talked
of what they'd eaten, the fact of food:

macaroni with little wedges of new
potatoes done with bay leaf and a little
olive oil, maybe just one
garlic sliver. Fresh smoked ham
sliced thin as writing paper, broccoletti

buttered and blessed with lemon. Sturdy
mozzarella. Bread with cracklings
peppered in its crust. A bowl of fruit,
a clear-eyed wine. Then something good to say
about it, and a sweet that ends the meal in laughter.

Sometimes the father's relatives would write
from Brucculino USA. News about the grandfather,
uncles, aunts, names sounding like a smudge
of smoke along the sea's horizon. And once
in a while came packages, good things to eat

like chocolate, chewing gum. All eaten,
all praised. All good for the appetite,
good for the breath. Up to date,
American. From food comes force for the brain
and the back, each from its own, fish or red meat,

peas or cabbage. Now the father really went
for fried foods, condiments. Salt, lots of pepper.
It was medical, they kept him warm in winter.
So they wrote the grandfather, and one day came
a giant tin of pepper from Brucculino USA.

"A & P is the one for health," grandfather's
letter said, "I even put it in my coffee."
So A & P, the pepper, came to be
a morning medication out of Epicurus.
Each of them put it in their coffee, on their bread,

and the father blessed with the grandfather's blessing,
"Cient' anni," how they all would live a hundred
years, with their blood and bone and muscles
peppery, strong, and warm. No fears
of illness, or of death. *As long as you live*

there is no death. But the day death comes,,
then where are you? You are no more.
So there, you see? No need to fear. And he pointed
to a pair of carpenter's apprentices carrying
a coffin, eating *pizza alla pepata*.

Sometimes they argued. What about?
Should girls eat pepper? Should their wine be watered?
What would happen if the fumes of the pepper
stoked the ruby furnace of the wine?
Or questions for a day of disputation:

wine is good for the blood, so if wine
makes the blood good, does good in the blood
make for good in the girl? Back and forth
the little balls of questions bounced
across their table, as bright generations of beans

and tomatoes, chickens, muscat grapes,
marched like soldiers into pot and oven,
plate and glass.
                    Then came the war.
No letters, no packages. Ration cards.
Father, a prisoner in Africa. The mother

picking weevils out of flour. Sons
to German labor camps and daughters
on the streets for food. First there was an armistice,
then invasion, bombing. Then liberation, then bombing
once again. A jumbled, five-year declension

ending in an ablative absolute of dehydrated
peas and powdered milk, black market
spam, Hershey bars. But in Brucculino USA
the aged grandfather, aunts and uncles prayed for them,
and the prayers were birds that flew among the fields

searching out the food. So it came one day
that the war was really over, and the birds
turned into letters, CARE packages.
The father and the sons came home. And there was milk
and lard, then butter, cheese and coffee.

Finally a package came from Brucculino USA.
It was A & P. And they sat with tears like tiny
onions glistening in their eyes. Life
was coming back. They could feel it flowing
out of that greatest place, America.

One day from Brucculino USA there came
a package, but no letter. Clothing, shoes.
Some towels and underwear. And buried in the middle,
a canister, taped and sealed. Carefully
concealed. Inside, they found it full

of darkish powder, that was all.
It wasn't pepper, father said. What could it be?
It must be something good. They sucked
their fingers, savoring. No one had a clue.
Maybe for the pasta, mother said, so she put

a spoonful in the water on to boil, and it seemed
to make the pasta sing. You won't believe it,
she exclaimed. They tried it, they all
agreed. It was something new. American.
Better than pepper, father said.

So start again, life did, started
with what was in the blood, old blood, but their blood.
You know the rest. You probably can predict
just how this ancient fable has to end.
A bowl of fruit, a clear-eyed wine,

then came the letter, weeks delayed.
One of the uncles wrote, "My dearest
brother, you cannot know how heavy
weighs my heart in writing you. Tell
your children that their grandfather died

serenely, in his sleep. Cremation, according
to his wishes. And did you get the package
with his ashes? See that they are buried
in our Naples. Your brother and your sisters
embrace you, through their tears. Cient' anni!"

So you start with what's in the blood. Old blood
but your blood. Meaning old hungers, reaching out
through a maze of streets and alleyways
where there's always a waft of eels dancing
in boiling oil and crusty loaves

of bread, browning under domes of ovens,
whispering *savor.* And *remember.* The two
together, whose sum remembered comes to be
your hunger. All your life, your hunger,
the hunger known in Naples by who bear it—

a boy who stands before you, begging,
a girl who scuttles in the shadows, crying,
a woman washing pearly coils of tripe,
a man who hawks a hamper full of dreams,
listening to that whisper...

ABOUT THE AUTHOR

Bruce Cutler's first book, *The Year of the Green Wave*, was chosen by poet Karl Shapiro in 1960 to start off the First Book poetry series of the University of Nebraska Press. Since then, Cutler has published ten volumes including his most recent narrative, *The Massacre at Sand Creek*, published by the University of Oklahoma Press in 1995. Nominated for a National Book Award, the book deals with the massacre of Cheyenne Indians by members of the Colorado militia at the end of the Civil War.

Cutler's poetry has appeared in publications including *Poetry, Poetry Northwest, Shenandoah,* and *New Letters*, and in eleven anthologies, including Morty Sklar's *Editor's Choice II*. He has appeared on the Studs Terkel show (WFMT, Chicago), and on David Ray's *New Letters on the Air* (syndicated). He has held a Bush Artist Fellowship (1990-1991), a National Endowment for the Arts Creative Writing Fellowship in Poetry (1989), and a grant from the Witter Bynner Foundation for Poetry (1986). Two of his verse plays have received Equity productions. Cutler is a graduate of the Iowa Writer's Program and was the founding director of the creative writing program at Wichita (Kansas) State University.